W9-BNL-619

Tigers

by Lesley A. DuTemple
photographs by Lynn M. Stone

Lerner Publications Company • Minneapolis, Minnesota

For my mom, with love.
        —LAD

For Brittany, who likes tigers as much as I do.
                —LMS

Photographs in this book were taken in Busch Gardens Tampa; Chicago Zoological Park (Brookfield Zoo); Cincinnati Zoo and Botanical Garden; Lowry Park Zoological Gardens, Tampa; Minnesota Zoological Garden; San Diego Zoo; and Ranthambhor National Park, India.

Thanks to our series consultant, Sharyn Fenwick, elementary science/math specialist. Mrs. Fenwick was the winner of the National Science Teachers Association 1991 Distinguished Teaching Award. She also was the recipient of the Presidential Award for Excellence in Math and Science Teaching, representing the state of Minnesota at the elementary level in 1992.

Additional photographs are reproduced through the courtesy of: pp. 12, 14–15, 21, 24–26, 31, 33–34, 42 © Anup Shah; p. 37 © Anup and Mahoj Shah; p. 32 © Sylvia Stevens.

Ruth Berman, series editor
Steve Foley, series designer

Library of Congress Cataloging-in-Publication Data

DuTemple, Lesley A.
   Tigers / by Lesley A. DuTemple ; photographs by Lynn M. Stone.
      p.   cm.—(Early bird nature books)
   Includes index.
   Summary: Describes the physical characteristics, habitat, behavior, and life cycle of tigers.
   ISBN 0-8225-3010-4 (alk. paper)
   1. Tigers—Juvenile literature. [1. Tigers.] I. Stone, Lynn M., ill. II. Title. III. Series.
QL737.C23D87 1996
599.74'428—dc20   95-32006

Manufactured in the United States of America
1 2 3 4 5 6 – SP – 01 00 99 98 97 96

Contents

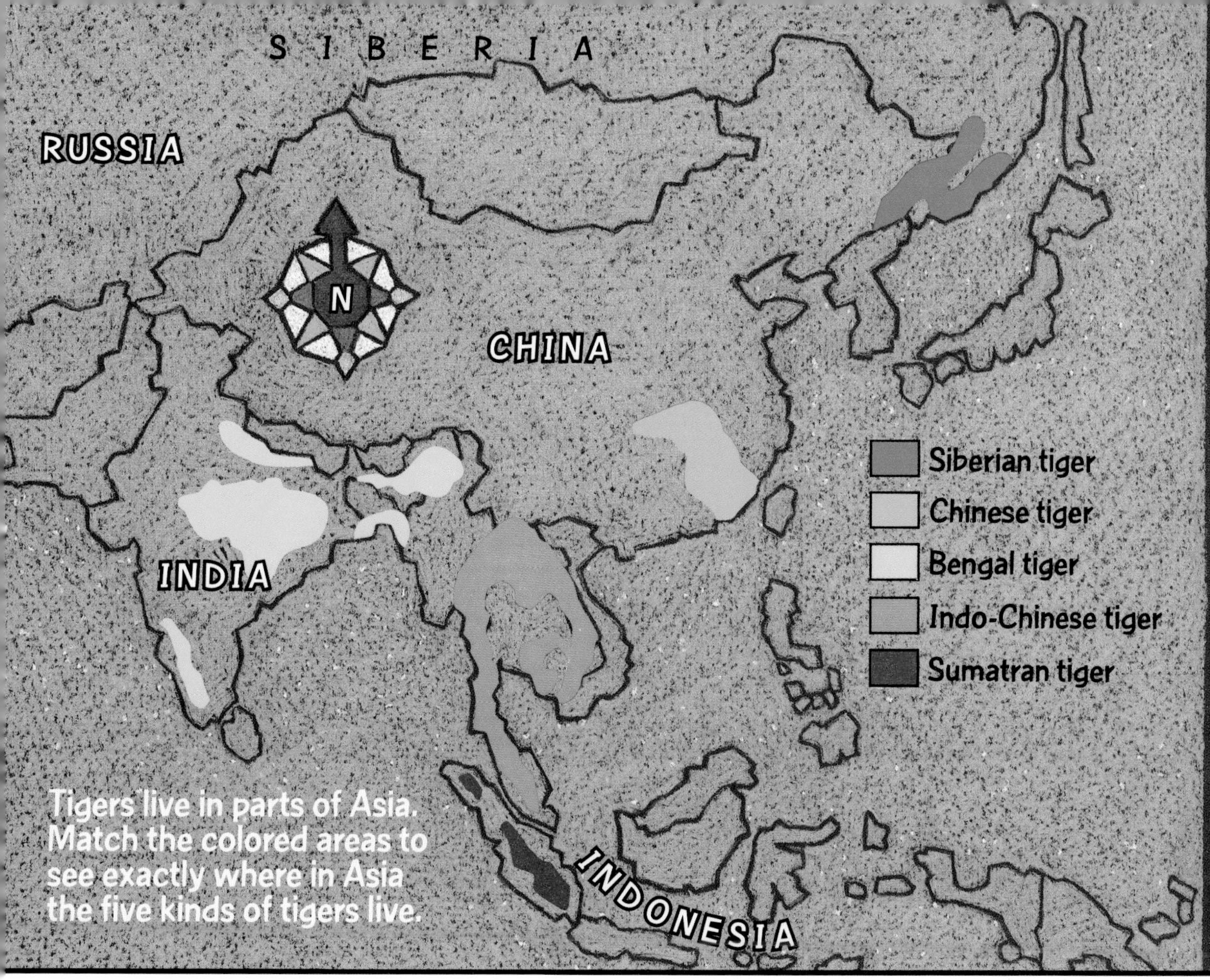
SIBERIA
RUSSIA
N
CHINA
INDIA
INDONESIA
Siberian tiger
Chinese tiger
Bengal tiger
Indo-Chinese tiger
Sumatran tiger
Tigers live in parts of Asia. Match the colored areas to see exactly where in Asia the five kinds of tigers live.

Be a Word Detective

Can you find these words as you read about the tiger's life? Be a detective and try to figure out what they mean. You can turn to the glossary on page 47 for help.

carcass
carnivores
den
endangered
extinct
habitat
litter
nursing
predators
prey
stalking
territory

Chapter 1

Some tigers grow to be 12 feet long and weigh 700 pounds. How fast do you think a tiger can run?

The Biggest Cat in the World

 What has claws and soft fur? And what purrs when it's happy? A cat. But what kind of cat can run 30 miles an hour? And what kind of cat can jump across your classroom in one leap? A tiger!

Cats are divided into three groups. The three groups are small cats, cheetahs, and big cats. There are many kinds of small cats. But cheetahs are in a group all by themselves. And there are only five kinds of big cats. The big cats are lions, leopards, jaguars, snow leopards, and tigers. Tigers are the biggest of the big cats. They are the biggest cats on earth.

The house cat is one kind of small cat. House cats and tigers are both members of the cat family.

Tigers can live in many types of land. They live in the snowy forests of Siberia. They live in the mountains of China. They live in

Some tigers live in places that are cold. Their fur grows thick and shaggy to keep them warm.

Other tigers live in warm places. The tiger's scientific name is Panthera tigris.

the jungles of India. Siberia, China, and India are all in Asia.

There are five kinds of tigers. They are the Bengal, Chinese, Indo-Chinese, Siberian, and Sumatran tigers. This Sumatran tiger lives in a good habitat.

Tigers are careful when they choose a place to live. The place where a kind of animal can live is its habitat. A tiger habitat has to have a lot of space. It has to have good places to hide. And it has to have plenty of food and water.

10

Water is important to tigers. Tigers don't like hot weather. When it gets hot, tigers like to get wet. The water helps them cool off. Tigers play in water, too. Most pet cats hate to get wet. But tigers are great swimmers. Sometimes tigers spend all day soaking in a river.

Tigers are good swimmers. A tiger can easily swim 3 or 4 miles.

Chapter 2

Each tiger has its very own territory. Do you think a tiger will share its territory?

Tiger Territory

 Many tigers live in a tiger habitat. But each tiger takes part of the habitat for its very own. This is the tiger's territory. The territory for one tiger is bigger than a small town!

Sometimes male tigers share their territory with female tigers. Sometimes female tigers share their territory with other females. But male tigers never share with other males.

Most tigers are orange with black stripes. But some are white with dark stripes. Most white tigers are born in zoos.

People build fences to keep others out of their yards. Tigers make a kind of fence too. They mark their territories. A tiger marks its territory by urinating on bushes, trees, and the

This tiger is about to spray urine on a tree to mark its territory.

The smell of urine tells this tiger that it is in another tiger's territory.

ground. When another tiger comes along, it smells the urine. It knows the land belongs to the other tiger.

A tiger scratches and rubs a tree to mark its territory.

Another way a tiger marks its territory is by
scratching tree trunks. The tiger stands on its
hind legs. It scratches a tree with its front
claws. Its claws make deep marks on the tree.
Sometimes the tiger scratches the ground, too.
When another tiger finds scratch marks, it
knows to stay away.

Tigers also roar to tell other tigers to keep out. A tiger's roar is very loud. If a tiger roared outside your school, the windows would probably rattle!

A tiger's roar can be heard 2 miles away.

Tigers don't always want other tigers to stay away. Sometimes they are nice to each other. When two female tigers meet, they're often friendly. They rub against each other and make purring sounds.

These tigers look like they are fighting. But they are really playing in the snow.

No one knows for sure why all tigers have a white spot on the back of each ear. Showing its white spots may be a sign that the tiger is upset.

But when two male tigers meet, watch out! They snarl, spit, and hiss. Sometimes they fight. A tiger will fight to keep its territory.

Chapter 3

A tiger can eat up to 70 pounds of meat in one day. What do we call an animal who eats meat?

How Do Tigers Hunt?

 Tigers need big territories. They need enough room to hunt for food. Tigers eat meat. Animals who eat meat are called carnivores (KAHR-nuh-vorz). Tigers are also predators (PREH-duh-turz). Predators hunt and eat other animals.

The animals that predators hunt are called prey. Tigers usually hunt large prey. They hunt wild pigs and deer. But they also hunt small prey, such as monkeys and frogs.

Sometimes tigers can't find large prey. Then they hunt small prey such as this monkey.

Tigers hunt alone. They usually hunt at night. Their eyes and ears help them hunt. They can see at night. And they can hear the softest noise.

A tiger is watching and listening for prey.

Tigers use their claws to hold food while they eat (left). *When the claws are not in use, they retract. Then they are hidden in the tiger's paws* (right).

Tigers have long, sharp claws. Each claw is as long as your finger. Scratching on tree trunks keeps claws sharp. Tigers use their claws to grab and hold prey. The claws retract when the tiger isn't using them. When claws retract, they pull back into the tiger's paws.

You can see the soft pads on the bottom of this tiger's paws. Pawprints can be used like fingerprints to tell which tiger made them.

A tiger's paws have soft pads. Most big animals are noisy when they walk. But the pads on tigers' paws help them walk without making a sound. Walking quietly helps tigers hunt.

Tigers in India often eat porcupines. This tiger is watching a porcupine and may pounce soon.

Tigers hunt by stalking (STAW-king). They sneak up on their prey. When a tiger sees a prey animal, the tiger crouches down. It hides in long grass. The tiger creeps close to the prey. Then it leaps forward and attacks the prey.

The tiger hits the prey with its paw. This makes the prey stumble and slow down. Then the tiger grabs the prey and bites its neck. The prey dies. The dead animal's body is called a carcass.

The tiger doesn't eat right away. It drags the carcass to a safe place. It hides the carcass

Tigers are strong hunters. This tiger is dragging a carcass to a safe place.

Strong jaws and sharp teeth are great for hunting.

so other carnivores won't find it. Then the tiger eats.

Tigers have sharp teeth. Their teeth are good for grabbing and ripping food. Tigers don't chew much. They tear off a bite of food, and then they swallow it. They eat until they are full.

A tiger uses its rough tongue to clean its fur and to lick scraps of meat from bones.

The tiger stays near the carcass and eats when it is hungry. It finishes a large carcass in about three days. Then the tiger licks the bones with its tongue. A tiger's tongue is rough and scratchy. The tongue scrapes the last bits of meat off the bones.

The tiger rests for a few days. Then it's time to hunt again. Hunting is hard work. But tigers only have to hunt about once a week.

A tiger may stalk 20 animals before it finally catches one. But then the tiger rests for a few days.

Chapter 4

Tiger cubs' eyes open when they are one or two weeks old. Where do you think this cub could have been born?

The Life of a Cub

A female tiger is called a tigress. Baby tigers are called cubs. A tiger family is made up of a tigress and her cubs.

When a tigress is going to have cubs, she needs a den. A den is a place that is hidden and safe. It may be in a cave. Or it may be under bushes. The den is where the cubs are born.

Striped fur helps a tiger stay hidden. This would be a good place for a tigress to have her den.

A litter is a group of animal babies. The babies are born at the same time. They have the same mother. There are one to six cubs in a tigress's litter.

People hardly ever see newborn cubs because the tigress hides them so well. This cub is two months old.

A tigress licks her cubs to keep them clean.

Tiger cubs are born blind and helpless. They're so small, you could hold one in your hands. The tigress stays close to her cubs. She moans softly to them. She licks them to clean their fur. Newly born cubs drink their mother's milk. This is called nursing.

There are usually two or three tiger cubs in a litter.

The tigress protects her cubs from enemies. Sometimes another predator finds the den. Then the cubs are not safe there. The tigress moves them to another den. She carries the cubs in her mouth, one at a time. She takes them to a safer place.

The tigress can't stay with her cubs all the time. She needs to eat. She covers the cubs with grasses. Even the smallest cubs stay quiet. Then she goes hunting.

When the cubs are eight weeks old, they are big enough to eat meat. The tigress brings meat to the den for them. The cubs stay in a den for two more weeks. Then they go with the tigress when she hunts.

Young cubs sleep a lot. When this cub is six months old it will be as big as a German shepherd dog.

Tiger cubs must learn to hunt. They watch their mother hunt. They practice hunting when they play. They stalk each other. They pounce on their mother. When they are six months old, they start to help the tigress hunt. When

Tiger cubs are playful. Playing helps cubs learn to hunt.

These cubs are almost as big as their mother. Notice how each tiger has its own pattern of stripes.

they are older, they can hunt small prey by themselves.

Tiger families stay together for two years. Then the cubs are fully grown. They must find their own territories.

Chapter 5

Tigers are big and strong. What do you think can hurt a tiger?

Dangers to Tigers

 Adult tigers don't have many enemies. But sometimes they get hurt when they hunt. If the prey has horns, the tiger can get cut. Or the prey may kick the tiger with its hooves. But prey animals don't usually kill tigers.

Tigers also fight with other tigers. They get scratched and bitten. Sometimes fighting tigers get hurt badly. Then they die.

But people are tigers' most dangerous enemy. For many years, people hunted tigers. People killed tigers for their beautiful fur.

The tiger's striped fur is beautiful.

Sometimes a lot of people hunted together. They killed many tigers at once. People thought this was great sport.

People also moved into tiger habitats. They hunted the prey animals. They cut down the trees. They left the tigers with very little food. There wasn't enough land for tiger

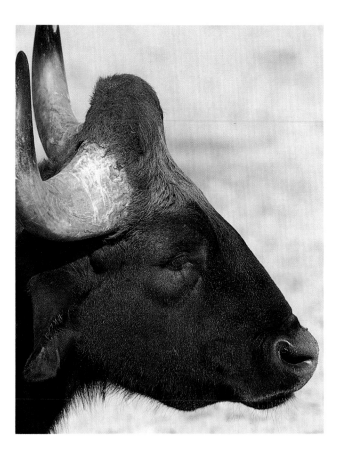

Both people and tigers hunt wild cattle. If people kill too many cattle, there may not be enough left for tigers.

If tiger habitats are destroyed, cubs like these won't be able to find territories to live in.

territories. There wasn't enough space for tigers to have families.

Now tigers are endangered. Many tigers have died, and not enough cubs are being born. Tigers may become extinct. Then there would be no tigers left in the world.

People in Asia have set aside land for tiger parks. The parks are big enough for tiger territories. People aren't allowed to hunt tigers there. The parks may help keep tigers from becoming extinct.

This tiger lives in a tiger park in India.

There are many tigers living in zoos. But very few tigers live in wild habitats. The tiger parks in Asia are helping more tigers live in wild habitats. With help from people, these big, beautiful cats can be around for a long time.

This tiger lives in Lowry Park Zoo in Florida.

On Sharing a Book

As you know, adults greatly influence a child's attitude toward reading. When a child sees you read, or when you share a book with a child, you're sending a message that reading is important. Show your child that reading a book together is important to you. Find a comfortable, quiet place. Turn off the television and limit other distractions like telephone calls.

Be prepared to start slowly. Take turns reading parts of this book. Stop and talk about what you're reading. Talk about the photographs. You may find that much of the shared time is spent discussing just a few pages. This discussion time is valuable for both of you, so don't move through the book too quickly. If your child begins to lose interest, stop reading. Continue sharing the book at another time. When you do pick up the book again, be sure to revisit the parts you have already read. Most importantly, enjoy the book!

Be a Vocabulary Detective

You will find a word list on page 5. Words selected for this list are important to the understanding of the topic of this book. Encourage your child to be a word detective and search for the words as you read the book together. Talk about what the words mean and how they are used in the sentence. Do any of these words have more than one meaning? You will find these words defined in a glossary on page 47.

What about Questions?

Use questions to make sure your child understands the information in this book. Here are some suggestions:

> What did this paragraph tell us? What does this picture show? What do you think we'll learn about next? What are the four things a tiger habitat must have? Could a tiger live in your backyard? Why/Why not? What would you need to live where tigers live? How do tigers mark their territories? How do tigers get their food? How is a tiger family like your family and how is it different? What do you think it's like being a tiger? What if there were no tigers? What is your favorite part of the book? Why?

If your child has questions, don't hesitate to respond with questions of your own like: What do *you* think? Why? What is it that you don't know? If your child can't remember certain facts, turn to the index.

Introducing the Index

The index is an important learning tool. It helps readers get information quickly without searching throughout the whole book. Turn to the index on page 48. Choose an entry, such as *claws,* and ask your child to use the index to find out how tigers use their claws. Repeat this exercise with as many entries as you like. Ask your child to point out the differences between an index and a glossary. (The glossary tells readers what words mean, while the index helps readers find information quickly.)

All the World in Metric

Although our monetary system is in metric units (based on multiples of 10), the United States is one of the few countries in the world that does not use the metric system of measurement. Here are some conversion activities you and your child can do using a calculator:

WHEN YOU KNOW:	MULTIPLY BY:	TO FIND:
miles	1.609	kilometers
feet	0.3048	meters
inches	2.54	centimeters
gallons	3.787	liters
tons	0.907	metric tons
pounds	0.454	kilograms

Family Activities

Have your child make up a story about tigers. Be sure information from this book is included. Have your child illustrate the story.

Visit a zoo to see tigers. How are they similar to other kinds of cats in the zoo and how are they different?

Watch a house cat playing with a toy. Notice how the cat stalks the toy and then pounces on it. Make a list of ways house cats behave like tigers.

Act out being a tiger. Where do you live? What do you do when heat bothers you? How do you clean your fur? How do you hunt for food?

Glossary

carcass—the body of a dead animal

carnivores (KAHR-nuh-vorz)—animals who eat flesh or meat

den—a hidden, safe place. Tiger cubs live in a den until they are about 10 weeks old.

endangered—having only a few of a kind of animal still living

extinct—having no members of a kind of animal still living

habitat—an area where a kind of animal can live and grow

litter—a group of babies born at one time in the same family

nursing—drinking mother's milk

predators (PREH-duh-turz)—animals who hunt other animals

prey—animals who are hunted and eaten by other animals

stalking (STAW-king)—hunting an animal by sneaking up on it

territory—an animal's very own place. A tiger marks its territory so other tigers will stay away.

Index

Pages listed in **bold** type refer to photographs.